The Disintegration Loops

The Disintegration Loops

poems

Stephen Cramer

SERVING HOUSE BOOKS

The Disintegration Loops

Copyright © 2021 by Stephen Cramer

All Rights Reserved

Published by Serving House Books
Copenhagen, Denmark and South Orange, NJ
www.servinghousebooks.com

ISBN: 978-1-947175-49-5

Library of Congress Control Number: 2021931107

No part of this book may be used or reproduced in any manner whatsoever without the prior written permission of the copyright holder except for brief quotations in critical articles or reviews.

Member of The Independent Book Publishers Association

First Serving House Books Edition 2021

Cover Design: Michael Balzano

Author Photograph: Holly Brevent

Serving House Books Logo: Barry Lereng Wilmont

Acknowledgements

The American Journal of Poetry: "Space Oddity"
The American Poetry Review: "The Disintegration Loops"
Barnstorm: "Spring Harvest"
Comstock Review: "Spelling B"
Connotation Press: An Online Artifact: "Muddy Tavern Blues"
          "Solder: A Debate"
Cortland Review: "One Night Stand"
Diode Poetry Journal: "Lipstick"
The Lake: "Key"
Manhattan Review: "Practicing"
Michigan Quarterly Review: "Coltrane's Teeth"
Ocean State Review: "Seven Signs"
Off Course: "Bank"
Pamplemousse: "Brush with a Dagger"
The Pinch: "Miracle"
The Salon: "Spur"
Southern Poetry Review: "Sistine Ceiling"
Statorec: "The Chase"
Third Mind: "Off Minor: Sonnets for Thelonious"
Yale Review: "Wanting the Buddha"

Also by Stephen Cramer

Shiva's Drum

Tongue & Groove

From the Hip

A Little Thyme & A Pinch of Rhyme

Bone Music

A Jar of Moon Air: Selected Poems of Jaime Sabines (tr. with Alejandro Merizalde)

Turn It Up! Music in Poetry from Jazz to Hip-Hop (editor)

The Hot Sauce Madness Love Burn Suite

For Joanna, Isa, & Chunker

Contents

I.

13 Lipstick
17 Mastodon
19 Wanting the Buddha
21 Coltrane's Teeth
23 The Beekeeper's Wife
24 The Muddy Tavern Blues
26 Tattoo Suit

II.

31 The Disintegration Loops

III.

47 Practicing
50 Space Oddity
53 Brush with a Dagger
57 Sistine Ceiling
60 Bank
62 Baboon
68 Solder: a Debate
70 Moonlight
73 Key

IV.

77 Off Minor: Sonnets for Thelonious
82 Spring Harvest

84 The Chase
86 Spur
89 One Night Stand
91 To an Athlete Dying Young
93 Miracle
96 Spelling B
98 Seven Signs

101 Notes

I

Lipstick

The knot of six or seven
boys dashed back & forth

against the strobe
of sun through pines, lipstick

slurred across their chins
& cheeks. I stumbled,

a few delirious streaks
crosshatching my brow,

across the stippled field
of corn plowed

under. We were far
past the ditch of poison

ivy & jewel weed, far
from the closest house

where, an hour before
we'd raided one of our mothers'

dresser tops for lipstick's
barrage of colors—

Tropic Sunrise, Chili
Burn, Wine-Dark Plum,

their names as lavish
as their hues. Then we ran

off to the woods
where we could rub

those shades onto the ends of our
swords—sticks, really,

a slew of bent
branches that we'd ripped

from live trees so that rot
wouldn't sneak up on us

mid-combat. Then
it was every shirtless boy

for himself, each waving his
sword, some with the precision

of a compass, others
as wild as a blind

dervish. As we lunged
toward each other, backed away,

lunged & retreated,
someone across the field

might have mistaken our moves
for an elaborate dance—glide

& stretch, turn & counterturn—
until finally, the sky dizzy

above us, we sprawled
on the matted gold

of grass, all of us slashed
& branded with sham

blood. After the heat
of battle, we'd check ourselves,

showing off with pride
a swath of unscathed flesh,

&: I got you there.
Yeah but I got you

there. Then we'd help
each other rub off

the scars, smearing the lipstick
into the various tones

of our skin. Not one of us
had yet received an errant

blur of lipstick
from another's mouth.

Though we might have bragged
differently, it'd be years

until our first real
kisses, & a few weeks

after that before our first
breakups. But here we were practicing

for all the wounds
we'd earn in the coming

years, & here we were,
all of us so eager

to go out & receive them.
So I want to hold on

to those days just before
the onslaught of all those

more lasting scars,
when we lay spread-eagled

next to each other, sweaty
with our own hurt & healing,

when we still couldn't tell
wounds from kisses.

Mastodon

Watch the world with both eyes,
& don't stop watching.
I was too busy grinding

the sun-rich mosses in my molars
to notice when the loam
grasped my ankles

with the ferocity of a sabertooth
but the patience of lichen.
By the time it reached my knees,

my frantic pawing only quickened
my slide into the boggy hollows
of the glacial lake bottom,

mud clogging my trunk
while I gasped for my last
knowledge of air. I couldn't conjure

the thousands of years
that would pass, each moment
as bloated as my cheeks

but quicker than a breath
while I shrugged off
my shaggy cloak & donated

my eyes to the soil.
As the old waters receded,
the earth turned squid ink

black against the tired
grid of my bones
until finally the farmers found me

in the drainage ditch,
their shovels kissing
the dirt of my lips.

When they swept the black away
they found me still standing,
only a few missing toes

that people had stolen for a lover's
trinket or the bottom
of a forgotten drawer.

But I don't mind. I'm a student
of the grand dispersal. What eats
will be eaten. What is nurtured

will nurture. I hope that the rest
of my herd made it to those
emerald slopes. I hope that they ate

until they couldn't eat, then rested
& ate some more. But time will make
patience of us all. I've learned

to be satisfied with the memory
of buttercups crammed
between my teeth & tongue.

Wanting the Buddha

Tired of the whale
so old his eyes are cataracts, tired

of the string-thin legs
of her purple-spotted cat

& the floppy bear,
its legs drained

of their downy filling,
Isa turns to the bronze

statue in the corner
before she goes to sleep.

I want Buddha, she says.
Silence, for a moment

as we three look
at each other. Then

Jo responds: *Buddha doesn't want
to be wanted.*

I smile. Good answer.
But then the ripples

of implication start
& don't stop.

Isn't not wanting a form
of wanting? I want

but don't want.
I think but don't say:

Buddha doesn't.
I'm right, of course,

but have never been
more wrong.

Coltrane's Teeth

If sweets decayed his teeth—
sugared cornbread, the candied

yam, all manner of dime
store plunder: butterscotch
disks, honey drops & peppermint,

lemon balls & root beer
barrels—if sweets decayed

his teeth until only rot clenched
to the mouthpiece,
his sound is *anything*

but sugar: in that cut
with Monk when he bursts in late

like the only party guest
you ever *really* wanted
to come, his sound is whiskey

stirred with a dull blade, rust
mixing with smoky amber,

a side of crushed chili
pepper, & vinegar rubbed into
a wound. Easy enough

to kick heroin, tobacco
& liquor, but he'd never

be able to quit the sweet
potato pie topped with whipped
cream. If sweets decayed

his teeth, then his ever widening
spiral of shattered notes (knock out

all my teeth by 30, take my
liver on your best silver
platter, yes Death, lick your fat

knuckles & give me
the prettiest shiner I ever

prayed for) his spiraling
fragments of notes turn it all into
something so sweet

I'd beg for it again & again.

The Beekeeper's Wife

Even from afar, your hands,

      stippled by tiny footprints

of gold, can shiver my skin

to life. All afternoon, you wear

        a living shirt, the ribbons

    of your voice unspooling

across the ridge as you repeat

    the incantation that opens tiger

lilies to deeper shadow,

the song that grinds soil & pollen

        into sweat. Your glance shivers me

    into a hymn, dares me

to wear what I fear.

    I open my mouth,

& my tongue speaks wings.

The Muddy Tavern Blues

It doesn't matter your selection.
In this joint, the jukebox turns greasy

silver into the slow eddy
of Mississippi mud, into blues riffs

known for making skirts
shorter, into gravel-throated

confessions that dismantle
the night & reassemble it

to the rhythm of their own
tide. Out back, the riverbed

is silvered with scales, a living
schist, a thrashing hoard of glitter

& blood. Wave after wave
of salmon, coiling

& uncoiling in the dark. Wave
after wave of this bass line

I know so well it disappears
like the taste of my own

tongue. Kiss my skin
& tell me what you find,

because I don't know what I am—
skin is more than salt, more

than boundary, & I can only tell you
that the most basic

laws—gravity, motion—
all turn untrue when you

loosen your scarf to a man
giving all his breath to drive

a moan through brass.

Tattoo Suit

I can step into attitude
or shed it
with this sham skin

aswarm with ornaments
& charms: the weightless
anchor on my forearm,

the choker of barbed wire
shielding my clavicle,
the inky blooms

climbing the trellis
of my ribs. It's thrilling
to slip so easily

into another's skin.
As I wander among half-dressed
vampires & ghouls,

& the poor mermaid
on my side stares
from her puddle of blue,

I feel for moments at a time
that I've entered the ranks
of the cool. I can almost feel

the intense desire of the biker-
turned-pirate at the bar
& the cat who just slinked

through the door with two felt
triangles for ears
to ask me over for a drink

so that we can more easily
revel in the camaraderie
of the branded. But before

they can gesture me closer
whatever momentum my blood
may have gained stalls

& I feel hollowed out,
phony: here on my chest
is a rune I can't translate,

on my shoulder a memorial
for someone named Sam
whose life—whose gender even—

I can only guess at.
A painless way
to get a tat, says the werewolf,

nodding at my nylon-sheathed
arm. The pixie & the cowboy
say the same with the requisite

jab to my ribs. But the longer
I'm in this skin, the more
I do feel pain. Not the fiery

pain of hot metal
etching into my flesh,
but the dull, more aching

pain that I'll never really get to slip
into someone else's skin.
I look down at my chest

& arms & wish. Then I walk
to the bar, allowing myself
to be remade. For tonight,

anyway, I'm bolstered
by the dragon helixing
my arm, I'm held up

by that dark tribal
weave on my neck, I'm purified
by that swirl of clouds

on my shoulder,
& I'm desperately in love
with a person named Sam.

II

The Disintegration Loops

i.

When I lit the furnace
in my cellar last
night, I stepped into

the cone
of its glow
as it spilled up

the stairs, kindling
the dark map of slime
mold that keeps

unraveling
across the drywall's
terra incognita. White

asterisks surf
the ripped insulation.
Dark whiskers

congregate like old
sages in the corner.
This basement's a garden

of spores & rot's drab
blooms. Somewhere down here
I'd stashed a few tapes

full of riffs I'd wanted
to show you twenty
years ago, before we lost

touch. I'd like to find
touch again. So I overturned
the place, searching

boxes & fingering
through the broken wings
of files. When I uncovered

the reels, I found
I was too late: they were already
flaking, the magnetic film

sifting to the floor like sepia
dandruff. I can't
imagine they still hold

any music. The score
will only breathe
in my memory.

ii.

*Memory is an unloyal
boomerang. The most accurate*

*recollection lays safe
in the warm coils*

*of an amnesiac's brain.
The rest can't help*

*but morph each time
they're retrieved. Save*

*what you can & save it
now. Each pulse is a lemming*

*blindly stepping off a cliff.
Not one of them hesitates*

*to follow the tail
of his older brother. Not one*

*looks back to see
the face of his younger.*

iii.

Those tapes from my younger
years: hearing them
again is like scratching

open an old
wound. Still, I followed
your advice & digitized

the reels. But looping
the riffs created
a result I didn't intend.

At first, the notes
surfaced just as
I remembered. Then, each time

through its circuit, the tape
shredded another note or
half a note, peeling like a snake

that needs to grind its old
skin into the grass.
The music—I'm not sure

how else to say
this—began to erase
itself from the air.

There's something dazzling
about hearing
your own creation devolve

back into the primal
hush, something absolutely
appalling about watching silence

eat its way
through the music
like moths into old silk.

iv.

*A six month old
kid crawls*

*toward seven
months. We're all*

*walking documentation
of erosion. Your music*

*became more real
the day it started*

*dying. Digitizing
(Ha! We old composers*

*never had such words)
those reels:*

*it's like chronicling
a dune as it's dismantled*

*grain by grain,
like getting intimate*

*with the biography
of a single crystal*

*of sand as it washes out
to sea. Relish it.*

*Life's the game
against entropy*

*you've already begun
to start losing.*

V.

The loops have started
to mess with me:
when I play them

I keep
thinking I'll pin down
the exact moment

when the music starts
disappearing.
But trying to catch loss

in the act is like
trying to lasso
your breath. I'm suddenly

useless, waiting
for changes I'll never
sense, a frog

in boiling water.
So I listen to the first
loop & skip

to the thirty-eighth.
Then I can plainly
hear the wearing

down, hear what notes
have been ground
away. Those that time

has spared keep on
as best they can.
The music falters

& staggers
forward. The broken
melody limps & surges on.

vi.

*Moldy lips
& empty eye*

*sockets. That's the station
we're all pulling*

*into. Don't believe
me? Take a photo*

*of yourself every morning
& hang it*

*on your wall. You'll see
no change from day*

*to day. But look in a year,
& you'll see the birth*

*of a wrinkle
hurtling like horizontal*

*lightning across your
cheek. Look in twenty*

*& you'll find your face
made of lightning. Forty*

*& the storm
of years will turn you*

*into its own
weather. Some days*

*I'm only made real
by touch. Mountains,*

*sky, plates of kiwi
& calabash leave me*

*stale. Even music washes
over, its intimacy*

*distant
as Timbuktu. Come visit.*

*In the meantime, I pray
to whatever drives sap*

*into branches & blood
into the tips of my toes.*

vii.

A trip's not in
the cards, but I thought
you'd be interested in this:

yesterday morning
as I listened to the end
of the loops where silence

outweighs the song,
a hailstorm was tearing
marble-sized holes

through the plants on my fire
escape. Ice
that was lodged

in the fleshier stems
disappeared
so that only the hole

remained. Fog uncreated
the angles of the sky-
line. Now, as eighteen

stars prick the night,
I think I feel
the leaden measure

of your loneliness. Nineteen
stars. The palisades
of clouds are dissolving.

Twenty. I'm sending
a copy of the loops
your way in the hope

that it can give you
some company
in my stead. Twenty-four.

viii.

*Some company for
these past few days*

*has helped. I usually melt
into the loneliness*

*between heartbeats.
But the rhythm*

*of your loops
fills the empty*

*spaces. Thank you
for your gift.*

*Our chests
make music before*

*we know what music is,
but the most*

*mature strain
is silence. They give*

*you a rattle
when you're born*

*so by the time
you sound your last—*

*saliva pooled at the back
of your throat—*

*you'll be consoled
by habit. All those*

*gathered around
will lean in, awaiting.*

*You'll have practiced
your whole*

life for this.

III

Practicing

Fistfuls of feathers stolen
from pillows, hot
pink & turquoise plumes

plucked from some unlucky
mother's boa, war
paint of smeared blush,

& necklaces strung
with mismatched beads:
our loot was vast

because we were all allowed
to scrounge for the block-wide battle
reenactment. But when we tried to help

the big kids assemble the costumes,
they banished us from the yard,
brandishing the snub nosed

crooks of sticks that they'd shaved
into pistols. When we stuck
around, our wobbling orbit

growing closer to the heat
of huddled boys, they turned
to different ammo. *How about you go*

practice dying, one of them said
to a storm of teenage
cackles. We turned away,

but not out of shame. The insult
meant to provoke us
instead made us swell

with purpose. Not everyone
could make it through
the mock battle alive. But if we had to go,

we'd go in *style*. So we spent
the rest of the sweaty
afternoon rehearsing: the heart-clutch,

the dizzy stumble & weak-kneed
slump to the ground, the wheeze
& grunt & final throat

rattle. We were Shakespearean
in our extravagance: stabbed,
we'd find it in our lungs

to unleash thirty lines of soliloquy
as the hill took our bodies
until we rolled to rest in the gutter

clogged with chicory & Queen
Anne's lace, a half a dozen boys
sprawled together, kissing

the ground with frozen stares.
Then, wiping the gravel
from our palms, the grass

from our hair, we got up & did it
again. But release
is the hardest-earned skill.

So the harder we tried
to fade from the world,
the more *of* the world

we became, feeling
for the first time the hidden
chill of the grass, the breeze

striding across our necks,
the maples converting
their sugars at the edges

of the lot. After thirty more
years of rehearsing, I lie
on a plot of dirt

& grass & look at the long
vault of the sky,
& I think of those pimpled

sages who taught us
so well, or at least set our feet
on the right path. We have such

a vast ground. We have a little
more time to practice. Little
by little we get this dying right.

Space Oddity

Ground into paste then mixed
with chamomile & verbena, the rhino

horns are guzzled as a cure for cancer,
their filaments leeching
pathogenic heat from the blood

so that it can glide, cool & pure,
from heart to toe & back.

Or, as a swank aphrodisiac,
they're passed around like roaches
at a party to grease the wheels

of foreplay. *Less death, more
sex*: marketing doesn't get more

effective. That's why the Jeep's stereo
bleats across the Serengeti,
the blue sky & torched earth

staring each other down like mismatched
eyes. Mark's driving because Becky

took a second longer to pull
on her boots, & Dave's rubbing sleep
from his cheeks as the homing

device quickens, its beeps
turning from a sprinter's heartbeat

to a continual whir
until the dip in the plain reveals
the rhino's hulk slumped in the red

dust. Dave & Becky are on the ground
before the Jeep even stops.

It's only been minutes since
the 2000 pounds of black rhino
had been darted from above,

but the tranquilizer skimming
through its blood won't last,

so as Bowie croons to *take your protein pills
& put your helmet on,* Becky tugs
the blindfold into place over its eyes.

The others finish fastening the rhino's
tree-thick ankles just as the helicopter

veers into view, its staccato peal slicing
Bowie's voice to a disjointed blur,
& before ground control can even declare

that *it's time to leave the capsule
if you dare,* the three have attached the cords

& given the pilot six thumbs up.
The helicopter clambers back into
the sky with the rhino hanging

from its underside like a dull pendant,
its toenails scratching the clouds. *I'm floating*

in a most peculiar way, Becky sings along,
& by the time Major Tom is drifting
in his tin can, the rhino is halfway

across the sky. By nightfall, he'll be pawing
new ground far from poachers,

& Becky & the boys, having just seen
something amazing—a rhino flying
as high as the most buoyant ember-flecked

warbler—will lean back between drinks
as the first few pinpricks

of light poke through the dark fabric
of the sky. *& the stars*
look very diff-er-ent today.

Brush with a Dagger

(Michelangelo Merisi da Caravaggio, 1571-1610)

i.

Bacchus (1597)

Overripe, the pomegranate
ruptures seeds to a bowl
of wilt & rot: worm hole
& bruise, ruined leaves

gone to rust. Even the gods,
in this city, can only afford
the picked-over, the second-
rate. His toga's draped to reveal

a laborer's pale cream
skin bleeding into sun-beat
wrist & neck. Not some
aloof deity, he's more wine

than cup, more tremor
than wine, his dirty fingernails
implicating him in the city's
labyrinthine networks of brawl

& vendetta: street boys,
prostitutes, bandits & thugs
making the perfect lineup
of swooning models for an angel.

ii.

The Conversion of Saint Paul (1601)

When the landscape warps
around the miracle,
the sudden anomaly's beheld
not by a milkweed

puff of overfed cherubs,
but by a horse's haunch—
let's face it, God's witness
is an ass—light falling

on gorged vein & taut
flesh, the accidental iron
omega of the raised
hoof. As the day's luster

slopes from lawless angles,
the shadows deepen
to a dusky coma & threaten
their easy embrace. But shadows

don't need to play up
their seduction, not when he so
stalks & hounds them
the way others seek light.

iii.

The Virgin (1605)

The Virgin, modeled
after a whore from Piazza Navona,
accused the artist of swapping
brush for knife the night

that one of her clients was stabbed.
Another week, drenched
in alcohol, the painter tossed
a plate of scalding artichokes

into a waiter's face, luring
a brawl through the door.
He claims that a questioning
sergeant had his skull

bashed in by a stone
dislodged from a rooftop.
But when he knifed
a man into a corpse over a lost

bet, he had to escape Rome
in disguise, so he donned
his models' robes & trinkets,
a murderer bolting in saint's garb.

iv.

The Execution of Saint John the Baptist (1608)

Prep work's shunned
for immediate culmination—skip
the charcoal for the scarlet
robes that almost outbleed

the Baptist's head. The blood
sprayed from the neck reconfigures
into the artist's signature: he, too,
is spilled, rent, hacked, far from the flush

body of Rome. When the trek
toward home is interrupted, old
wounds gather & pool
their weight. Prowlers turn

on him. The beach at night
is delirium… The church's aisles
blur to a dull haze. You have to squint
to find the forms made of dusk

& whiskey's amber. Feed the slot
its coins, & they reach out, they linger
like a vendetta, they gain on you.
Then it all plunges back into shadow.

Sistine Ceiling

A quarter inch behind the 343
        absurdly muscled bodies
pours a river of sky, the blue

vault misted by the cosmic sequins
           of stars. Piermatteo d'Amelia's night
                shimmered for twenty years

until it was plastered over
        with the regimented sweep
of a history: light peeled

from darkness, serpent & eviction,
           the rush of life touched into
                that comatose finger...

Another divine encounter: when Krishna
           revealed to Arjuna his true form—
planets & pulsars unlimited, waves

upon waves of moons—the vision
           stretched reason till it fizzled,
                till the god mercifully contracted

back into the comfort of lips & limbs.
        Himalayas, oaks, oceans,
& yaks all crowded back into a mustard

seed, & each of those billions of galaxies
           was replaced by a blade of grass
                on that long stretch of field.

No wonder we restore the cracks
       in the ceiling's cornice
& pilaster. We take comfort

in the crawl of history—
       how petroglyphs of crushed
            berries & dirt give way to

the microchip, how Jurassic
       reptiles press on to Renaissance
artists & the first woman

to Mars. Those first days in 1508
       when the scaffold angled
            its planks to the ceiling

& a sculptor began stroke
       by stroke to plaster over
his sky, what would Piermatteo

have thought? *Some asshole
       is painting over my design.* Or maybe
            the sudden erasure would have let him walk

the city of vendors & cobblestones,
       of lemons & figs & thieves,
& feel the harefooted

shiver of something rushing
       behind it all—call it mystery,
            void, heaven—something

more deeply interfused,
       forever concealed,
but because of that, more radiant

& terrifying. Look into the void
       for too long & you'll be begging
            for the earth back. Maybe

Piermatteo would've thought *one day, someone's going to*
 paint over his work, & he'll see
how it feels. Or maybe,

as the light splintered down
 on the statesmen & grandmothers
  jostling for the ripest

persimmons & the sweetest
 plums, he'd have found that—
 covered, shrouded, eclipsed

by the story of human
 push & scramble—his work
  became even more true.

Bank

Nickel & rupee, centavo & baht
tossed for good fortune

into a Thailand fountain
turned cataclysmic in the stomach

of the green sea turtle—subsequently
(& lamentably) nicknamed "Bank"—

a resident at a *conservation* center,
no less, in Sri Racha. Shine & shine:

too much shine to resist,
even for this animal whose fare

usually consists of seagrass & algae,
& this new metallic diet

has grown heavy: five pounds
of human grease & sheen

in her stomach, making it
easier to sink than swim,

the exaggerated dig of the front
flippers, the strain toward the surface

for air, the ventral shell fractured
under the weight, splitting

under each stroke. General
anesthesia & a four-inch incision:

five surgeons withdraw 915
coins from Bank's stomach.

The blank eyes out-torpor torpor
as the slot regurgitates

metal, catching the relentless light.
All she can see is vague figures

swaying above, the way the stream
of conservatory visitors

used to ripple & wrinkle
through the water's veil.

Baboon

The girl stepped out
of her boyfriend's car,

a pashmina coiled around
her face, & entered the current

of students hauled into the school
by the auditory yank

of the morning bell. Heads turned
to the scarf's helix

of turquoise & cinnamon
dappled here & there with flecks

of gold, its two bangles
overhanging the slit

the girl had left for her eyes.
She knew the accessory

would kindle a remark or two,
but at least in the halls

she could always hurry
past. Once she reached

the bondage of her classroom seat,
though, the cold planks

of students' stares collapsed
to so much gossip

that the teacher slammed
down her pen in the middle

of attendance, stood behind her desk
as though a flagpole

had replaced her spine
& asked the girl to *please*

take off your scarf.
When the girl hesitated,

the teacher—thinking *I will not
let the day unravel*

at 8 AM—added *unless you want
detention, young lady.*

The girl looked back & forth
as though she were about to cross

the widest, busiest street
in town, then she lifted her hands

to her head & slowly began
the work of unraveling.

The room went as silent
as the June sky as the girl

parted her scarf to reveal
not the small scar

that some had grown to suspect
but a completely purple

face: lilac blooms across her
cheeks, wine-dark dendrites

on her chin. Even her nose
& forehead, those sitting closest

noticed, were stippled with plum.
Then, five heartbeats

into the sight, the insults
began to bruise

the air: *Smurf*, a boy hissed.
Baboon laughed the girl

who the day before had been known
as the second prettiest in the room.

The teacher, overwhelmed,
made herself grab the girl's forearm

& hurried her down the hall.
The first thing the nurse did

was wipe the girl's face
with a cloth, expecting paint,

expecting makeup. When it didn't
rub off, she recoiled

& was about to take
the girl's pulse just to give

herself some time to think
when she noticed the one place

where the purple bled
into the natural cream

of the girl's skin.
Is it possible, she said, making

herself look at the girl,
that this is a hickey.

The girl fell back into the closet
of her own hands

& wouldn't explain, no matter
who tried to coax her,

how the night before,
jealous of the way the rest

of the world got to take
in her beauty—her Cosmopolitan

cover-shot complexion,
the perfect golden ringlets

of her locks—her boyfriend had sucked
on her face, breaking blood

vessel after blood vessel,
how hour after hour

he had meticulously joined
all those small islands

of bruises until
they were one continuous

continent that stretched
from ear to chin to ear.

Ashamed, how could she admit
that she just sat there

on his couch, sticky
with what she'd want to call

his love, as he stained her
with her own blood

until she'd grown purple
with possession.

As the skin on the girl's
thighs clung to the nurse's cot,

the teacher handed back her scarf
as though to say, *now I see.*

Go ahead. Cover up.
But by that point the scarf

could never be big enough
to cover the girl's shame.

At the moment she couldn't think
beauty is interior, couldn't think

*he's shallow, I have to move on,
I will heal.* The best she could do

was imagine a Pashmina big enough
to wrap not just her head but her

whole body, yes, that was it:
she needed ribbons

& ribbons of color cascading
from her head to her toes, the thread's

embrace so snug to her skin
that nothing—no grasping fingers,

no muscle-bound arms, no, not even
the strongest vice in the world—

could ever hold her so tight.

Solder: A Debate

> —After a man in Zimbabwe transformed
> a machine gun into a saxophone.

If a garden has an opposite,
it's this: hoards of sun-baked
firearms breaking through
the sand, the stalks of barrels
leaning into the wind,
ammo sprinkled about
like golden seeds.

Rejiggered, the gun's barrel
can be pummeled
into the goose-neck curve
of a saxophone's peak.

Heaps & heaps of guns
are buried all over this desert,
the grim harvest of sixteen
years of civil war.

The trigger & pistons
can be doctored into keys.

When gunfire dismantles
the flight of lilac-
breasted rollers scissoring
the dusk, we find the closest
basement & repeat whatever
prayers we can remember.

I found the AK47
angling out of the earth

*& disassembled it.
Then, like beating a sword
into a plowshare, I soldered it
back together until its hollow
was made for holding
breath.*

You can't fight the enemy
with a concert.

*The shoulder stock can
be converted into the bell's
tubular bloom. The magazine
can be hammered
into a mouthpiece.*

Weapons help the enemy burn
partitions into the sand.

*This twisted metal wants
to sing, & singing can cluster
even the most far-flung clans.*

This shifting sand is full
of partitions.

*I lift the burning
to my lips.*

Moonlight

I've got the moon in my blood,
Damon says. That's why
he's been in the same bed

for the past three months, counting
pigeons out the window or being tugged
along by the continuous paper traincars

of his comics. *What kind of moon*,
I ask as I empty his trash, *a full one
or a slice?* Kids in this hospital

open up to me because custodians
don't carry needles. *The slice*, he says.
But he prefers to talk about superheroes

& their powers. *Can people fly?* he asks.
I glimpse the contents of his comic's
pages. *You mean like Batman?*

Damon frowns. *Batman can't really fly.
He's just got cool gadgets.* I nod, schooled.
Because if I could, he says, *I'd fly*

*right outta here & search the universe
until I found a place where the moons
in my body could grow so full*

*that the light would burst right through
my skin.* His words punch the air
like a fist to a villain's jaw.

Then he raises his eyebrows.
You know what the universe is, right?
I smile. *I've heard of it.* I mop the last

of the floor with a few smooth figure-eights.
I've spent enough time here
to know that *sickle cell* can make for some short

coffins. So that summer when it came time to wash
the hospital's windows, I suited up in the rented
costume & stood on the roof, the wind

whipping my black cape like the flag
of a fictional country. I strapped the harness
around the black spandex, adjusted my mask,

& rappelled down the building's side
with my bucket, spray bottle, & squeegee.
When I spotted Damon's window—

easy enough with the knot
of action figures sprawled
against the glass, I quickly dropped

the last few feet & splashed suds
across the pane. Damon, who must have seen
just a dark silhouette blurred

by the cataracts of froth, sat bolt upright
in bed until I wiped the pane clean
so that he could look directly into the eyes

of the caped crusader.
He didn't seem to mind
that his hero had traded filaments

of webs for the spray from a plastic
bottle, because he wrapped his blue
blanket around his shoulders

like a cape &, as I swabbed the pane clean,
rubbed his side of the window
as though a clear stretch of glass could defeat

all the villains in the world. When I'd finished
the window I stood there feeling silly,
a breeze working its way under my skin,

& I'm not sure what I expected to happen next.
I gave the rope some slack & plunged
through the air, my cape billowing

around my shoulders as I dropped
to the next floor. Thanks to Damon, I know
that it was Bruce Wayne's limitations

that made him come up
with all those life-saving gadgets & wings,
but I'm not sure why I dressed up or

what it was worth. Oh hazy articulation,
oh cloaked meaning. Yes, we are tethered.
& our tethers can help us fly.

Key

I don't know what makes
your breath more song

than song. I don't know how
to teach my hands

to still or how dragonflies
find the frail link

which binds two bodies
to heaven & the underneath.

I don't know why
as soon as you're born

you're old enough
to get dead or

how long the dog can bark
at his own echo.

I don't know why
the sign behind the bar

says: *If you ain't got nothing
to do don't do it

here*, because nothing is what
I'm trying to learn

how to do. I know my body
awaits me, cold,

at the end of a leash,
but I don't know how

many years long
that leash is, studded

with its misshapen pearls.
I don't know why

the world dropped a skeleton
key at my feet,

but you better believe
my hand is at the door.

IV

Off Minor: Sonnets for Thelonious

i.

The network of fissures clips the opposite

      wall, cleaves the cornice to splintered

garlands. So you'd think, especially in this light,

      that the bar's ruptured Victorian mirror

would ruin the concert's already

      static display. But somehow, shattered

to deeper precision, it actually

      perfects Monk's hunched figure blurred

across the TV—his beret's slim shadow

      cutting the dark gleam of his shades,

          the insistent, angular pulse of his shoes.

          The mirror's perfectly busted to match the bruise

of hammered bass notes, quick arpeggios

      inverted to staccato cascades.

ii.

Minor chords: 1958's Indian

        Summer. The sun, pelting Interstate

95, cancels the median,

        torching Nica's Bentley like hate

as she chauffeurs Monk to a Baltimore gig.

        The day all sweat & fever, they pull

off for a cold one, Monk stretching his legs

        in the bar while Nica cuts a butt outside. Small

town, so she's just grinding one out against

        the pavement when she hears the siren's whine.

Two cops pull up & step inside. It's then

        that she notices the hand-lettered sign

by the door—*whites only*. Too late: the men

reappear, Monk expressionless between them.

iii.

Monk's resigned. But when the cops try to duck him into

        their cruiser, something snaps: he grasps the door,

braces his six-foot frame, & no words will move

        him. The sun pierces the two silver

              badges. One of the men makes a quick

hand-motion toward his hip...

                      No: before

I envision what these two officers

        would do to make him submit, my mind cuts back

to the footage of Monk's hands laddering the keyboard

        in a broken, off-minor blur

              of flatted fifths. I admit: the memory of this

            solo is a smoke-screen, a useless

diversion to help me not see the cops' abuse

as they billy-clubbed those furious fingers loose.

iv.

Ruptured flesh: my white
                face is splintered

    by the bar's mirror,
                even as its glass doubles

        the bottles below
                like a mini Manhattan

echoed in the Hudson's mud.
                The concert's over.

      Over the years as I've imagined
                Monk's knuckles

swollen past syncopation,
                I've been of two

      minds. Now I feel that no
                art is worth that pain,

that I'd skip all those
            nights of listening to

    save him from
            that burn. The other

    hurts to admit: years ago I thought
                let the cops batter

      their impotence
             on his skin. Let them

      strut their sarcasm.
                Let them tighten

those cuffs just enough
                              to keep on

shattering him
                    back into song.

Spring Harvest

After a long

        winter, when I dig

my fingers into the cold

frame's still ice-bound

        soil, I find in my hands

    the bone chips

that some sated animal

    has left behind

& the sharp hulls

of seeds. When I sift

        the dirt out & drop

    the shards

into a tin bucket

    reserved for weeds

& other vagrants

I expect dissonance, a metallic

    quarrel of birth & end.

    Maybe it shouldn't scare me

that I can't tell them

    apart, that they make the same

bright & fearless rattle.

The Chase

I hate that the word
I spilled in anger is still
traveling away from us

into space, particles
striking each other
in a commute unending,

a mini comet
with my fury as that tiny
pinprick of fire out front.

When my body's gone,
I'll still be the record
of all the words I say—

that slow, irregular
Morse code rippling out
to the stars. But some day

millennia from now,
some unfathomable
life form may catch,

in their alien equivalent
of an ear, my future
long since past—how,

with my next words,
I hunted down that ridiculous
quarrel, how I trailed it,

shadowed it past pulsars
& through asteroid belts,
far past our galaxy's

milkiest rim. I hope,
whoever might overhear this,
that they're as patient

as you, my sweets,
that they don't turn away
before they hear how I sent

the smallest emissary
of a kiss stowed in a capsule
of whispered syllables

to hazard those hurling
fires uncharted,
that unnamable dust.

Spur

Heirloom necklaces
                twisted into pearled
     helixes & figure-eights

          as they were vaulted
over the monastery
         walls. Flocks of coins

vollied forth like light
            spilling upward. 1347,
Lubec, Germany: monks

         barred their gates to avoid
the plague,
         but the crowd, gathering

against dusk, still gave up
           rings & lockets, tossed
full purses, even shoes

         to appease the God
who sent them this Black
       Death. They'd become animals

in their hoarding
         & now were animals,
maniacally squealing.

         But moments later—no one
could've expected it—
      it was all flying

toward them again. The monks,
        fearing disease, threw the fortune
    right back. For hours, the sides

        hurled belongings
  back & forth
        until, muscles sore

with relinquishing,
        the monks gave up,
    & the riches piled

        waist-high inside. It's hard
to imagine—these days of ads
        in the jungle, commercials

in the Congo—giving all your strength
        in a battle
    not of conquest

        but of riddance,
cleansing yourself item by item
     of all that holds you

to the world. We're told
        & told what to want until we do,
    & again we've made ourselves

        a cult of want,
& we move within our web
        of things. I don't want

to know what catastrophe
        or pestilence it'll take
    to stop us. But never mind.

   Just ask your possessions
  where they're going
    tonight. Then put down

your shaggy hooves
    where they point you.
  They'll burden your back

    & you'll feel the spurs grind.
  Things are in the saddle
   & ride mankind.

One Night Stand

Baby, I'm gonna love you
till the moon

turns white, till rivers run
downstream, till rocks

mature into knots
so hard they can break

a man's bones or teeth.
Honey, I'm yours

till birds learn the trick
of flight & lizards

scratch their bellies
on sun-

baked desert stones.
No lie: nothing

can stop us
till last week's fruit

goes bad, till
the tides turn

twice a day.
I'm all yours till

my errant heart
beats double-time

& the yellow eyes
of the ever-gazing

sun break
over the constant hills.

To an Athlete Dying Young

      for Jason Horner (1974-2006)

I first read Housman's famous poem
in high school, when you were busy

with your fast break into the lane,
roll off the fingertips, kiss

the backboard & swish.
You'd probably never heard of it,

how it glorifies the youth who dies
before he can watch his name

gradually buried by those who break
his records. You broke

a few those seasons, would've broken
more. But senior year, they discovered

your delinquent heart, & you had to sit
the bench. That week, sports stripped

from you & your certain future
dissolving, you said *Sometimes I just sit*

& wonder what's going on.
Then your usual cocky head tilt

pressed on to the angle of pure
perplexity. *Is that philosophy?* Though

it occurred to me, I never showed you
Housman's verses. Because let's face it,

all its fame can't make that damn poem
right. Dying young—how would you

have said it?—*sucks*, & whoever
says differently says wrong. Jason,

it's true: so many of us
want our legacy to last long after

we're gone. But tonight, I hope
we all outlive our names.

Miracle

Nothing out of the ordinary
in the middle of this pedestrian

bridge except that I'm early
for work, & the lotus-posed

monk in the saffron robe
is hovering two feet off the ground.

As tourists gather, one kid,
who seems to be weaving his way

toward some unknown fix, is suddenly
riled up by the constraint of gravity.

He jumps. He crosses his legs mid-leap.
&, before he can close his eyes

with the facade of serenity, falls
back to the ground with a clatter

of knees & elbows. Confounded,
he swipes his hands beneath the monk's robes,

searching those thick folds for hidden
supports, but he finds only a flimsy cane,

which barely seems to touch the sidewalk
beneath him. He bangs the pavement

with his fist, as though the bridge itself
were the source of his failure.

Those who were snapping shutters
& turning the monk's silver

bowl into a miniature gong
with their coins, back off.

The monk himself sees none of this.
He keeps his eyes shut as though any

interruption could send him crashing down
from his spindle of air. Hours later,

when I'm heading back home, & the last
orange columns of the sun slur across

his shaved head & the water's skin below,
I catch the monk settling back down

to earth, revealing his trick: a steel rod
runs from a cushioned seat beneath

his robes, through his hollow cane,
& is anchored into a large metal plate

beneath his prayer mat. The work day over,
the man pulls off his robe to t-shirt & jeans

& slips off his latex scalp
to expose a full head of hair. The last

stragglers turn away, disappointed,
their coins sticking to their pockets

as if they hadn't known that gravity,
that ruthless master, in the end owns us all.

But the faux monk's work isn't done
eeven when he packs up & leaves,

because all day questions bled through the city:
Did you see that guy on the bridge?

Did you get a photo? How's that even
possible? Seam & seem:

in the places we come together,
things aren't what they are.

& that's okay. Fool me. Tell me another
unbelievable tale. Ask any scientist how,

& she'll have her theories. Ask her why
& she'll shut up, & then you'll know

the reason we tell stories, the reason why
that supporting rod & plate don't matter,

because we're held together
not by what we know

but by what we don't,
because a man was sitting on the air.

Spelling *B*

Decked out in strange medallions,
the whole bus of kids was sporting
pint-sized chalkboards—the kind

the deaf might hang from their necks—
for the make-shift game: I'd say
a word, & they'd spell it out,

raising the boards like gold
medals. One girl—two braids
down her front, a big toothy

grin, a cane across her lap—
was curiously consistent.
For the task of *apple*,

she wrote: *b b b*, for *dog*:
b b b, the letters shaped
with attention, erased then

shaped again for the next round.
&, though she wouldn't talk,
she always asked with her eyes…

I'd just smile. *You'll get the next one.*
I knew it was a lie,
knew it could be years

before she improved, if at all.
But why *should* she improve?
At least on that bus trip

we could celebrate the crooked
roads of her letters over
precision. We pulled up to the school

in time for one last word:
*can anyone here spell
buh-buh-buh?*

& she chalked it out
to a flush of surprise.
I raised her arm in triumph,

but I knew even then
it was a silly gesture.
I should've taken her hand.

I should've taken her
aside. I should've spoken to her
in her own tongue

until all she was able to say
spread out to explain everything:
Just be, child. Just be. *Just be…*

Seven Signs

i.

*Burlington Beverage
& Redemption*: bring us your
empties & be filled.

ii.

The sign just off school
grounds is a fine message for
our kids: *Do Not Pass*.

iii.

Stenciled on each train
car's rear: *No Humping*. Mind your
own business, Train!

iv.

Anxious hospital-
bound cars shift from 60 to
10: *Patients Only*.

v.

The church's sign says
I am the door. But it's not
the door. It's a sign.

vi.

Danger: Falling Ice.
Mid-July, a child looks up,
anxiously waiting.

vii.

The unfinished sign
at the cemetery's edge
simply reads *join us.*

Notes

"The Disintegration Loops": The circumstances of this poem, though highly fictionalized, have their basis in fact. The history of the piece of music known as "The Disintegration Loops," by composer William Basinski, bears repeating. Basinski's creation, which was recorded on a series of audio tapes in the 1980s, was badly stored. When he rediscovered the tapes twenty years later, he went to digitize them, but as he did so they began to flake. In an inspired move, Basinski looped the tapes so that the listener would hear the same phrases over and over. But as the tapes continued to revolve, silence invaded them from the inside. By the final loop, the listener hears not the soaring music of the beginning, but an homage to loss and stillness.

The poem makes large leaps from there. The two figures in the poem, the young composer and the older composer, are purely fictional. They have nothing to do with Basinski or the actual circumstances of finding the music.

This poem is for Jeff Oishi, who introduced me to Basinksi's work.

"Practicing" is for Mike B.

"Brush with a Dagger" is for Christina.

"Sistine Ceiling": Piermatteo d'Amelia was the first to paint the Sistine Ceiling. His painting was covered by Michelangelo's masterpiece.

"Moonlight": The circumstances of this poem are inspired by the day that employees from Allegheny Window Cleaning dressed up as superheroes when they washed the windows of the Children's Hospital of Pittsburg.

"Spur" ends with a quote from Ralph Waldo Emerson's "Ode, Inscribed to William H. Channing."

Stephen Cramer's first book of poems, *Shiva's Drum,* was selected for the National Poetry Series and published by University of Illinois Press. *Bone Music,* his sixth, won the Louise Bogan Award and was published by Trio House Press. He is the editor of *Turn It Up! Music in Poetry from Jazz to Hip-Hop.* His work has appeared in journals such as *The American Poetry Review, African American Review, The Yale Review,* and *Harvard Review.* An Assistant Poetry Editor at *Green Mountains Review,* he teaches writing and literature at the University of Vermont and lives with his wife and daughter in Burlington.

www.ingramcontent.com/pod-product-compliance
Lightning Source LLC
Chambersburg PA
CBHW022013120526
44592CB00034B/796